How To Stop Being Manipulated

The Ultimate Guide on How to Handle Manipulative People

Patrick Smith

All rights reserved. No part of this publication may be reproduced, distributed, or transmitted in any form or by any means, including photocopying, recording, or other electronic or mechanical methods, without the prior written permission of the publisher, except in the case of brief quotations embodied in critical reviews and certain other noncommercial uses permitted by copyright law.

Copyright © Patrick Smith, 2024

Table of Contents

Chapter 1 5
Understanding Manipulation 5
    Symptoms of Manipulation in a Relationship 5
    Why Manipulators Act as They Do 9
Chapter 2 10
Recognize your vulnerabilities 10
Chapter 3 13
Setting Boundaries 13
    Types of Boundaries to Consider 14
    Communicating Your Boundaries clearly 15
    Maintaining Firm Boundaries 16
    Coping with Guilt and Emotional Blackmail 16
    The Function of Self-Care and Support Networks
    17
    Strategies for Enforcing Boundaries 18
    Managing Backlash from the Manipulator 19
    When to Seek Professional Help 20
    Maintaining Long-Term Boundaries 21
Chapter 4 22
Developing Assertiveness Skills 22
    Ways to Be More Assertive 24
Chapter 5 26

Developing Self-Esteem 26
    Examples Of Great Self-Esteem 27
    The Advantages of High Self-esteem 29
    How to Develop Self-esteem 30
Chapter 6 35
Fostering Healthy Relationships 35
    Navigate Social Situations With Confidence 36
    Tips For Developing Healthy Partnerships 38
Conclusion 42

Chapter 1

Understanding Manipulation

Manipulation occurs when someone uses mental distortion and emotional exploitation to persuade and manipulate others. Their intention is to gain power and control over others in order to achieve their goals.

Someone who manipulates you knows your weaknesses and will exploit them. If the person practicing the manipulation is receiving what they want from you, the manipulation will continue until you decide it needs to stop and actively and deliberately put an end to it. This can be difficult, and you should seek help during this process, especially if you are dealing with a consistently manipulative person.

Recognizing manipulation in your own relationship might be tough because it may have started out mild. Manipulative behavior in relationships might eventually become the norm with your partner.

Symptoms of Manipulation in a Relationship

If someone repeatedly makes you feel emotionally exhausted, nervous, scared, or unsure of your own needs, thoughts, and feelings, you may be subjected to emotional manipulation. When determining what is going on, trust your instincts. It may include any or all of the following techniques:

Gaslighting
A gaslighter may lie to you, blame you for things, and belittle how you feel. Gaslighting manipulation could include comments such, "You're insane," or "You're too sensitive."

Someone who gaslights you attempts to make you believe that you are unworthy of expressing yourself and that your feelings and emotions are not genuine or acceptable. People use gaslighting to reject any wrongdoing and establish control over what they think and do.

If you suspect someone is gaslighting you, pay attention to how you feel after spending time around them. You may feel confused, dissatisfied with yourself, inadequate, or unable to trust yourself.

Passive-aggressive Behavior
Passive-aggressive behavior, as opposed to straightforward speech, does not reflect how a person is truly feeling. Your partner may employ avoidance methods, such as purposefully avoiding you or avoiding discussing specific things. Sarcasm can be another indicator of passive-aggressive communication.
For example, a passive-aggressive individual may attempt to gain attention by making unnecessarily dramatic gestures such as sighing or pouting. They might utilize immature emotional reactions to trick you into asking them what's wrong without actually stating anything.

Lying and blaming
Someone who is emotionally manipulative is inclined to avoid taking responsibility for their actions. They may outright lie or exaggerate in order to portray themselves in a more positive manner. They may even transfer the blame onto you, making you question yourself and what happened. Though many of us tell "white lies," or lies we deem harmless, an emotionally manipulative individual would most likely tell lies to mislead you.

Threats and coerciveness
Someone who coerces you into doing anything by making threats or employing force is emotionally manipulative. For example, your partner may threaten to leave you if you don't do exactly what they want.

Your partner may threaten you by stating they will hurt themselves. They use the danger of self-harm to persuade you to do what they want. They may or may not injure themselves, but self-harm should never be taken lightly.

You can encourage your partner to seek therapy while maintaining any boundaries between you and them to ensure your emotional and physical safety.

Withdrawal & Withholding
Another indicator of emotional manipulation is when your lover withdraws from you. Perhaps they give you the quiet treatment if you are doing something they do not want you to do.

They may withhold information, attention, or even sex to "punish" you, even if the offense is minor. They may refuse to stop withdrawing or withholding until you comply with their demands or acknowledge culpability for something you did not cause.

Isolation
Someone who wants to dominate you may try to break off communication with friends and family, especially if any of your loved ones detest or distrust the emotionally manipulative individual.

On the other hand, an emotionally manipulative individual may attempt to earn the support of their family and friends for their personal gain. For example, if your partner knows you plan to leave them, they may try to persuade your family or friends to encourage you to stay with them.

Your spouse might try to cut you off from your network of friends and family, which would make you second-guess your decision to break up.

Implications of Manipulation

- *A persistent urge to defend oneself*
- *A lack of safety in the partnership.*
- *Lack of trust in your partner.*
- *A strong sense of self-doubt.*
- *Frequently apologizing, especially if you believe you did nothing wrong.*
- *Frequently experiencing perplexity, dissatisfaction, hurt, resentment, rage, weariness, and frustration.*

❖ *Overall dissatisfaction with the partnership.*

Honesty versus Manipulation
Emotional manipulation can manifest itself in subtle or blatant ways, but it is always detrimental to your relationship, confidence, and self-esteem. Here's a comparison between manipulative tactics and a healthy, direct approach.

Manipulation
  ❖ *If you loved me, you would join me at the movies tonight.*
  ❖ *If you don't pick up the kids, you obviously don't care about them.*
  ❖ *I would like to chat with you about anything, but I know you don't have time for me.*

Honest Approach
  ❖ *I want to go to the movies tonight. Would you like to travel with me?*
  ❖ *Please let me know if you can pick up the kids from school tomorrow.*
  ❖ *We should discuss some things when you have time.*

The examples above involve guilt-tripping tactics, such as insinuating that you don't love or care about your children because you don't execute particular things. Statements like these are attempts by the manipulator to embarrass the target into doing what they desire.

An example of a passive-aggressive statement is, "I was willing to speak to you about something, but I know you don't have time for me anyway." A manipulator may fear that you do not care about them, but instead of expressing this simply and honestly, they avoid the problem. They may belittle you in order to get an apology or make you feel horrible about a situation.

The purpose of manipulation is to exert control over another individual in order to achieve one's desired outcome. It can encompass a wide range of actions, ranging from the overt to the subtle.

Why Manipulators Act as They Do

In general, people manipulate others in order to acquire what they want, preserve their ego, and avoid having to accept responsibility for the repercussions of their actions. They may feel compelled to punish, control, or dominate their partner. They could be looking for sympathy or attention, or they could have other selfish reasons. They may also try to modify or wear down a partner in order to satisfy their own wants.

People who exhibit deceptive behavior in relationships may originate from a dysfunctional household. They might have needed to be coerced to get their basic needs met or to escape severe punishment, or their parents might have emotionally coerced them and taught them social skills through experience and observation.

People with attachment disorders and high levels of anxiety may be more likely to engage in emotional manipulation. In some circumstances, manipulative behavior is associated with indications of a mental health issue, like borderline personality disorder (BPD) or narcissistic personality disorder (NPD).

Chapter 2

Recognize your vulnerabilities

Understanding who we are and what motivates us is an essential component of self-knowledge. When we are clear about our beliefs, values, strengths, and shortcomings, we are better able to make decisions using our own criteria. However, when we lack self-awareness, we seek others for affirmation and advice, making us vulnerable to manipulation.

One of the reasons it is easier to manipulate people who are unaware of themselves is a lack of discernment. When we don't understand our own needs and desires, we're more likely to accept others' ideas and suggestions without scrutinizing their validity or intentions. This renders us open to manipulation since we are eager to absorb information and make decisions without critical thinking.

In addition, a lack of self-awareness can result in low self-esteem and confidence. People who do not know themselves want external praise and validation, making them more vulnerable to manipulation. Manipulators can take advantage of people's need for approval to achieve their own goals, whether by selling unneeded things or spreading damaging ideologies.

A lack of self-awareness might make it harder to detect manipulative approaches. When we are oblivious to our own emotions, limits, and wants, it is more difficult to detect when someone is attempting to influence us or exploit our vulnerabilities. This puts us vulnerable to manipulation without even realizing it.

People who know themselves, on the other hand, can create appropriate boundaries more effectively. They understand what is essential to them and can make decisions based on their personal well-being and values. They are less vulnerable to external pressure and can say "no" when something does not meet their own wants and aspirations.

So, how do we resist manipulation through self-awareness? The solution comes in devoting time and effort to discovering our own identity. This entails focusing on our views, values, and objectives, as well as being open to self-reflection and personal development. We can also seek assistance from therapists, coaches, or support groups to aid us with this process.

Finally, self-awareness is essential for preventing manipulation. When we understand ourselves, we are better able to make informed judgments and reject external influences. Understanding our own needs and actions enables us to establish healthy boundaries and protect ourselves from manipulation. People with a lack of self-awareness, on the other hand, are more vulnerable to manipulation since they seek approval and instruction elsewhere.

Lack of self-awareness can show in a variety of ways. Some people may struggle to identify their emotions and grasp how they affect their decision-making. Others may have a distorted self-image, making them more susceptible to manipulation by others looking to exploit their anxieties. Furthermore, a lack of self-awareness can lead to the adoption of self-destructive behaviors or the development of restrictive mental patterns, allowing others to manipulate you.

Manipulation takes advantage of our flaws and limitations. Manipulators use subtle tactics to manipulate our emotions, capitalizing on our anxieties, insecurities, and unfulfilled needs. If we do not know ourselves, we are more likely to fall victim to these manipulative tactics since we are not aware of the warning indications and are more easily misled.

People who know themselves, on the other hand, have a firm foundation from which to make informed decisions. They realize their own talents and weaknesses, as well as what is most important to them. This enables them to sift information and external influences, resulting in decisions that are consistent with their values and aims. Furthermore, those who know themselves tend to be more confident in their own decisions, making them less vulnerable to external manipulation.

So, how can we increase self-awareness and defend ourselves from manipulation? Here are certain steps we can take:

Practice self-reflection
Spend time examining your thoughts, emotions, and experiences. Ask yourself difficult questions and be honest about your strengths, faults, and desires.

Seek diverse perspectives
Listen to and consider other people's perspectives and experiences. This will allow you to extend your perspective and better comprehend your own values and ideas.

Establish healthy boundaries
Learn to say "no" when something does not align with your needs and aspirations. Do not be swayed by social pressure or manipulation from others.

Seek help
If you believe you require assistance in improving self-awareness, try obtaining advice from a therapist, coach, or mentor. They can give you the tools and assistance you need to develop your self-awareness.

In summary, self-awareness is critical for protecting ourselves from deception. When we understand ourselves, we are less likely to be swayed by others' hidden objectives. Understanding our emotions, beliefs, and values allows us to make educated judgments while protecting our autonomy.

Chapter 3

Setting Boundaries

Setting boundaries is an important part of any healthy relationship, particularly when dealing with manipulators. Boundaries help us establish our comfort zones and how we want to be treated by others. They are critical for maintaining respect and dignity in relationships, especially when dealing with someone who is prone to deceptive conduct.

Boundaries provide a framework for how we expect to be treated and what behaviors we will not tolerate. They contribute to a sense of safety and predictability in encounters. When limits are clearly defined and respected, the relationship becomes healthier and more balanced.

In the context of manipulation, borders serve as a protective barrier. They allow people to establish control over their emotional and physical spaces, preventing manipulators from overstepping. Setting boundaries is a sort of self-care that promotes one's mental and emotional well-being.

However, establishing limits is not always straightforward. It takes self-awareness, clarity, and confidence to declare oneself. It can be especially difficult in manipulative relationships since the manipulator may fight or disregard these boundaries. Despite these hurdles, defining limits is a significant step toward personal empowerment and freedom.

It's crucial to remember that limits aren't about changing the other person; they're about defining the parameters under which you interact with them. Boundaries are about accepting responsibility for your own well-being and refusing to let others damage it.

Finally, although defining boundaries is vital, so is enforcing them. Boundaries without enforcement are ineffective. Consistency in maintaining boundaries sends a clear message to the manipulator about what is and is not acceptable, eventually leading to healthier dynamics in the relationship.

Types of Boundaries to Consider

When creating limits with a manipulator, it is critical to understand the many sorts of boundaries that can be used. These encompass emotional, physical, temporal, and intellectual boundaries. Each type has a distinct purpose and covers various aspects of contact and personal space.

Emotional boundaries
These are intended to protect your feelings and meet your emotional requirements. These boundaries assist in determining how much emotional impact individuals have over you and in what manner. It entails limiting how much information you share about your personal life and how others can communicate with you.

Physical limits
These refer to your personal space and physical comfort levels. This can include regulating who can touch you and how, as well as determining your presence in specific contexts. It's about respecting your own body and finding comfort.

Time Boundaries
It entails planning how and with whom you spend your time. This includes making time for yourself and selecting how much time you spend with others, particularly those who may be manipulative. It's all about prioritizing your wants and responsibilities.

Intellectual limits
These refer to your thoughts, ideas, and beliefs. They entail respecting your own and others' rights to hold opposing beliefs and ideas. Setting these limits means not allowing others to ridicule your ideas or impose their beliefs on you.

Understanding these types of boundaries aids in successful communication and enforcing them in relationships, particularly those involving manipulative behavior. It's about striking a balance that considers both your wants and the dynamics of the partnership.

Communicating Your Boundaries clearly

Effective communication is essential for setting limits with a manipulator. Clarity, directness, and assertiveness are crucial communication skills. This entails clearly establishing your boundaries in a way that allows no space for misinterpretation or manipulation. Clear communication involves communicating your demands and limitations without ambiguity or reluctance.

When communicating limits, use "I" phrases to indicate how specific behaviors affect you. This technique asserts ownership of your feelings and experiences, making it more difficult for the manipulator to disagree or dismiss your viewpoint. Saying "I feel disrespected when you dismiss my opinions" is more effective than "You always ignore me".

In your speech, avoid using the words justify, argue, defend, and explain. Manipulators frequently employ these strategies to keep you in lengthy talks and wear down your determination. Maintain your boundaries without feeling compelled to justify or explain them excessively.

Nonverbal communication also plays an important role. Your body language, tone of voice, and eye contact should all communicate confidence and assertiveness. This emphasizes the importance of your boundaries and your determination to enforce them.

Finally, prepare for pushback. Manipulators may react badly to boundary setting. Maintain your composure and reaffirm your boundaries as often as required. Remember that setting limits is not a negotiation; it is about claiming your rights in the partnership.

Maintaining Firm Boundaries

Setting clear limits with a manipulator necessitates consistency and resilience. Manipulators frequently test or push against predetermined boundaries, therefore being firm is critical for their effectiveness. This includes continually enforcing your boundaries whenever they are challenged.

Staying solid entails identifying and opposing manipulative attempts. Recognize whether someone is using emotional blackmail, guilt-tripping, or gaslighting, and reply coolly by setting limits. It is critical not to engage in disputes or be swayed by emotional responses.

Self-care is essential for keeping firm limits. It increases your emotional resilience, making it simpler to remain firm. Mindfulness, therapy, or simply engaging in enjoyable activities can all help to strengthen your sense of self and resolve to preserve boundaries.

Seek help from friends, family, and support groups. Having a network of individuals who understand and support your efforts can be motivating and validating. They can also provide a perspective outside of the deceptive relationship, allowing you to remain grounded in your beliefs.

Finally, remember that it is acceptable to change your boundaries as needed. Life evolves, as do relationships. What matters most is that these changes are motivated by self-care rather than manipulation or pressure. Maintaining your boundaries is a dynamic process that requires ongoing self-reflection and change to preserve your emotional and psychological well-being.

Coping with Guilt and Emotional Blackmail

Setting boundaries with manipulators can be difficult due to feelings of guilt and emotional blackmail. Manipulators frequently utilize guilt to violate your limits and maintain control. Recognizing and resolving this approach is critical to your emotional wellness.

Manipulators are skilled at instilling guilt, which is a powerful emotion. They may insinuate or proclaim outright that you are selfish, indifferent, or a nasty person for establishing limits. It's critical to understand that this is a manipulative method, not a reflection of your personality or goals.

To combat guilt, reaffirm the reasons for your boundaries. Remind yourself that you have the right to maintain your emotional and physical health. Reflect on previous instances in which a lack of boundaries resulted in poor outcomes, emphasizing the significance of maintaining them.

Emotional blackmail is typically accompanied by guilt. Threats, ultimatums, or emotional outbursts may be used to persuade your decision. Even if you are experiencing emotional outbursts, remain cool and reinforce your boundaries. Remember that you are solely responsible for your own actions and well-being, not for the feelings or reactions of others.

Seeking aid from friends, family, or a professional can be quite beneficial in dealing with guilt and emotional blackmail. External opinions can bring clarity and affirmation, allowing you to stand firm in your decisions and resist manipulation.

The Function of Self-Care and Support Networks

Self-care and support networks are essential in establishing and maintaining boundaries with manipulators. Self-care techniques increase your mental and emotional resilience, making it simpler to set boundaries and deal with manipulative conduct.

Self-care activities aim to improve your physical, emotional, and mental well-being. This might be everything from exercise and a healthy diet to mindfulness practices, hobbies, or simply making time for oneself. Regular self-care relieves stress and enhances your ability to deal with difficult situations.

Creating a solid support network is also essential. Supportive friends, family members, or peers who understand your position can offer emotional support, counsel, and a feeling of community. They can provide a unique viewpoint on your relationship dynamics, allowing you to see things more clearly.

Participating in support groups, whether in person or online, may be quite beneficial. Connecting with individuals who have had similar experiences creates a sense of community and understanding that is difficult to find otherwise. These groups can provide practical assistance and coping skills based on their common experiences.

Therapy is another critical component of self-care when dealing with manipulators. A therapist can help you understand and manage your emotions, create effective boundary-setting skills, and cope with challenging circumstances.

Finally, remember that self-care and getting help is an ongoing process. It is critical to continually evaluate and change your self-care habits and support networks to ensure that they match your changing requirements and circumstances.

Strategies for Enforcing Boundaries

Enforcing boundaries with a manipulator might be difficult, but there are practical ways that can assist. Consistency is essential; limits must be enforced whenever they are tested. This clearly indicates that you are serious about your boundaries.

The broken record approach is an excellent strategy. Regardless of how the manipulator responds, continue to repeat your boundary in a calm, strong manner. This strategy avoids delving into reasons or justifications, instead focusing on the border itself.

Using time-outs can be beneficial, particularly when emotions are high. If the manipulator begins to overstep limits, temporarily withdraw from the situation. This not only gives you an opportunity to regroup, but it also shows the repercussions of boundary transgressions.

Documenting encounters can be useful, especially in cases where gaslighting or denial are common. Keep track of when your boundaries are tested or breached. This is useful for personal validation or when you need to involve authorities or specialists.

Seeking external intervention is another option. In some circumstances, hiring a mediator or professional might help to strengthen boundaries. This is especially important in extreme situations or when personal safety is at risk.

Positive reinforcement when limits are respected can also be beneficial. Recognize and appreciate courteous behavior. This can create a positive loop and demonstrate that polite behavior leads to positive relationships.

Finally, be prepared to re-evaluate and change your boundaries as needed. People and their situations change with time. What matters is that these changes be done from a position of strength and self-care, rather than manipulation or pressure.

Managing Backlash from the Manipulator

When setting limits with a manipulator, it is common to experience backlash. When limits are established, manipulators may respond with rage, guilt, or emotional outbursts. It is critical to plan for and effectively deal with this backlash.

First and foremost, remain calm and composed. Emotional responses might aggravate the issue. Keep your replies measured and focused on your limits, not the manipulator's conduct.

It's also crucial to keep perspective. Remember that the backlash is a reaction to losing control, not a reflection of your behavior or worth.

Reaffirm your reasons for setting boundaries, with a focus on your well-being.

Seek assistance at times of backlash. Friends, relatives, or a therapist can offer emotional support and keep you grounded. They can provide reassurance and remind you that setting boundaries is both good and important.

Finally, you should prioritize your safety. If the backlash turns into threats or actual violence, take proper precautions to protect yourself. This could include contacting authorities or seeking safe shelter, remember that your safety is the top priority.

When to Seek Professional Help

Seeking professional treatment is critical when dealing with a controlling relationship, there are some situations in which the advice of a therapist or counselor is essential. If you are continually exhausted, anxious, or sad as a result of your relationship, it may be time to seek professional treatment.

Professional assistance is also advised if you see a pattern of exploitative relationships in your life. A therapist can help you understand the root reasons for these habits and devise techniques to avoid them in the future.

If you have trouble setting and keeping limits, a professional can offer advice and assistance. They can help you build the skills you need to assert yourself and stay healthy in the face of manipulation.

Seek aid if the manipulation turns into physical abuse or threats. In such instances, it is vital to consult professionals who can assure your safety while also providing the necessary support and resources.

It's critical to remember that requesting help is an indication of strength, not weakness. Recognizing that you require assistance is the first step in taking care of your mental and emotional health.

Finally, if you are feeling isolated or unsupported, get professional help. Therapists can provide you with a nonjudgmental environment in which to examine your feelings and experiences, as well as support that you may not find elsewhere.

Maintaining Long-Term Boundaries

Maintaining boundaries over time necessitates consistent work and self-reflection. It is critical to reassess your boundaries on a regular basis to ensure they continue to meet your requirements and ideals.

Continuous self-care is essential for long-term boundary preservation. Participating in activities that promote your mental and emotional well-being can help you remain robust to manipulation.

Maintain your support network. Having a strong network of friends, family, or a support group provides continual encouragement and perspective, allowing you to stay committed to your boundaries.

Finally, keep in mind that maintaining boundaries is a constantly developing process. As you mature and your circumstances change, so will your boundaries. Regularly examining and changing your limits is an important component of personal development and maintaining successful partnerships.

Chapter 4

Developing Assertiveness Skills

Being assertive is speaking with others in a straightforward, honest, and courteous manner, without sugarcoating your message or acting forcefully and aggressively. Assertive behavior in partnerships can promote healthy communication in the following ways:

Help your spouse understand your boundaries, requirements, and wants. Inform others about what you like and dislike, so they can better understand you and support your requirements. Permit each partner to have a mutual understanding of their connection.

When someone is proactive, they articulate their needs or wants clearly, reducing negative results such as defensiveness, cognitive distortion, and misunderstandings. When you express your opinions, demands, or desires clearly and concisely, you are assertive. When we declare something to our partner, for example, we state it directly but also respect and consider others.

Assertive language is respectful yet not exaggerated. Overstating our position will undoubtedly increase defensiveness, whereas understating it will result in resentment. Furthermore, assertiveness should not imply aggression or harshness. When someone is aggressive or harsh, they may issue ultimatums, use force or threaten others, be disrespectful, or speak in a threatening, unpleasant, or disrespectful manner.

While aggression can be one-sided, assertiveness is properly expressing oneself while acknowledging that the other person has boundaries and rights of their own. However, society frequently categorizes assertiveness based on gender. Being aggressive transforms you into a real person with genuine perspectives, beliefs, and ideas. And that is not masculine or feminine, but simply human. Assertiveness enables people to:

Self-advocate
Directly stating that you want to date someone or what type of relationship you want. Telling someone you want to date them or indicating how serious or open you want the relationship to be will help you get the information you need from them. Then, regardless of the reaction, you'll know where things stand, providing clarity and reducing unnecessary concern.

Calling out when something bothers you or when you require assistance from your partner. There is so much repression of actual feelings, desires, and expectations that people are often surprised or uninformed of how the build-up occurred. When you are aggressive and listen to their point of view, you can reach an agreement that works for both of you.

Having unpleasant conversations when you have a need that is not addressed. Avoiding subjects that annoy you about your partner or relationship may seem safe at first, but it can be harmful. When we utilize communication, such as passive aggression, we are avoiding what we mean to communicate, thinking that our other will simply understand. While we avoid the difficulty of being direct, we are likely to wind up in a downward spiral with our spouse. The following methods for navigating uncomfortable conversations:

Concentrate on one issue at a time
Choose the appropriate time to address it when you are calm and your partner is receptive.

Preface your discussion of a sensitive topic with a positive perspective and examples of how you believe you can work together to solve it.

Set ground rules for interaction, and if things get heated, allow each other time to self-regulate before re-engaging.

Telling your partner what you actually want, not simply what you don't want. While it's easy to get caught up in criticizing others' behaviors, explicitly articulating activities you want and appreciate may enhance the likelihood of them occurring. Telling others what you appreciate when they do it allows you to express your appreciation while also providing straight and helpful feedback on what you enjoy and would like to see more of.

No one, no matter how long you've been together, can read your mind. When we express what we want immediately, precisely, and respectfully, it adds positivity to the connection.

Ways to Be More Assertive

The following are some tips for being more forceful.
Understand your present communication style. To do anything different, we must first understand what we are doing. Once you've determined what you want to improve, establish a personal goal to learn more about how to be assertive in relationships.

Practice, practice, practice. Assertive communication gets easier the more you practice it. It may seem unpleasant at first, but the more you practice flexing this muscle, the closer you will go to becoming better at asking for what you want, need, and deserve, which will increase your pleasure. The following methods to practice:

- *Keep a journal to document your development.*
- *Schedule time to exercise assertiveness.*
- *Say "no" more frequently to things you don't want to do.*
- *Express yourself, even if it is uncomfortable.*
- *Make a list of phrases you wish to incorporate into your assertiveness lexicon and share it with your partner.*
- *Increase your ability to tolerate discomfort through good tension or friction, which may occur when you express yourself assertively.*

Accept setting limits as a sign of self-love and a lesson in how others should treat you. To be more aggressive in our relationships, we must first understand our own personal boundaries. Once you've established your boundaries, it's easier to express your needs and desires to your partner.

Seek assistance from a mental health professional who can coach you in being more assertive.

Assertiveness in partnerships can promote healthy communication. Being assertive may not come naturally to everyone, but with practice, you can learn to become more assertive.

Chapter 5

Developing Self-Esteem

How do you feel about yourself? What are your thoughts on your qualities, characteristics, and identity? If you have a favorable view of yourself, you may have high self-esteem.

Simply expressed, self-esteem is how you feel about yourself. It differentiates between self-confidence and self-worth.

Self-esteem
This depicts your long-term perception of your skills, abilities, and attributes.

Self-confidence
This refers to your belief in your own ability or the understanding that you have the necessary skills to complete a specific activity or situation.

Self-worth
This describes how you perceive your own worth and value as a person. In general, having high self-worth means believing you are valued and deserving of respect, affection, and belonging.

Feeling less confident in some situations does not inevitably lower your self-esteem. For example, you may lack confidence when beginning painting classes yet believe you will learn rapidly. After all, you've done well in every previous art class, and you're confident in your ability to create art in general.

When someone harshly abuses your artwork, you may feel comfortable setting boundaries with them and dismissing their opinion because your self-esteem tells you that you deserve to be respected.

However, a lack of self-esteem can have an impact on your confidence in your abilities as well as your sense of self-worth. What is the good news? If you lack self-esteem, you can definitely work to improve it.

Examples Of Great Self-Esteem

If you have a high level of self-esteem, it will probably take a lot to undermine your confidence.

At school
Consider how you would react if you overheard someone mocking your attire or the ideas you offered in your literary class. If you have strong self-esteem, the teasing is unlikely to bother you because it has no effect on your internal opinion of yourself.

If you have poor self-esteem, you may take those remarks to heart. Perhaps you start to question your understanding of the short story. Or, when you arrive home, you take off your once-favorite attire and put it in a bag to donate.

At work
As another example, suppose you have a difficult work project. You've put in a lot of effort, but your results don't quite match what your supervisor expected.

If you have strong self-esteem, you are unlikely to internalize your lack of achievement or interpret it as evidence that you are lousy at your work or inept. Instead, you may go back to your supervisor, acknowledge you're stuck, and ask for some recommendations.

In relationships
Self-esteem can also play a role in relationships, especially when a partner mistreats you. It can be simple for you to confront your spouse when they try to undermine your self-worth, stand up for what makes you great, reject their taunts, and ultimately end a toxic or violent relationship.

Long-term verbal or emotional abuse from a partner or another loved one, on the other hand, can quickly erode your self-esteem. You may come to believe them when they declare no one else will want you or that you deserve their harsh treatment.

People frequently associate narcissism with extremely high self-esteem, yet high self-esteem is possible even without narcissistic personality disorder (NPD) or any narcissistic features.

First and foremost, it is critical to recognize that NPD is much more than just having high self-esteem and people with NPD are likely to have:

- *A sensation of superiority.*
- *Grandiose or exaggerated dreams about their capabilities and qualities*
- *A strong belief that they deserve admiration and attention.*
- *Decreased empathy for the feelings of others.*

Furthermore, while persons with NPD may appear to have great self-esteem on the outside, they may actually be vulnerable and insecure on the inside. People with high self-esteem do not feel empty and value themselves, in contrast to narcissists who frequently experience internal hollowness and emptiness.

According to 2020 research on how to raise children with high self-esteem but no narcissism, there are several differences between children with narcissistic features and those with high self-esteem.

Children who are narcissistic tend to:

- *Have unrealistically favorable, inflated, or elevated views of themselves.*
- *Aspire for greatness, in short, they want to rise above their colleagues and stand out from the crowd.*
- *Having a fragile self-concept that easily fluctuates between shame and overconfidence*

Children with high self-esteem typically:

- *Have optimistic but realistic attitudes about themselves.*
- *Strive for self-improvement and personal development.*
- *Believe in themselves, especially when faced with hardships or disappointments.*

According to the experts, parents can help their children develop good self-esteem by:

- *Prioritizing growth over supremacy, or emphasizing that learning is more important than outperforming others.*
- *Providing accurate and kind remarks rather than excessive or meaningless praise*
- *Make sure your children know you love and cherish them unconditionally, not simply when they do something.*

Even though this study focused on parents parenting children, you can apply the lessons to yourself. To put it briefly, no matter what, it never hurts to treat oneself with love, concentrate on improving, and honestly assess your talents.

The Advantages of High Self-esteem

High self-esteem can be a key component of overall well-being and mental health. Indeed, data suggests that strong self-esteem is associated with improved mental health and overall quality of life. According to 2022 research on the different benefits of self-esteem, increased self-esteem may lead to improvements in:

Social Relationships
Higher self-esteem may increase your likelihood of seeking connections with individuals who appreciate you as much as you value yourself, resulting in higher relationship pleasure. Furthermore, having high self-esteem may help you deal with rejection in relationships.

Performance in school
As a natural result of having high self-esteem, you may feel more motivated and engaged, increasing the likelihood that you will be invested in studying and finishing your assignments.

Performance at work
High self-esteem may improve your connections with coworkers and increase the likelihood that you will persevere when presented with problems, resulting in more job satisfaction and success.

Mental Health
Higher self-esteem may reduce your odds of developing mental health issues such as depression or anxiety, in part because you are less inclined to ruminate. This practice of focusing on the same gloomy, undesirable, or disturbing thoughts can contribute to both anxiety and depression.

Physical Health
High self-esteem can indirectly improve your physical health since it frequently leads to strong, supportive social interactions. However, the review authors emphasize the need for more investigation.

Antisocial Behaviors
High self-esteem may also make you less inclined to engage in antisocial conduct, such as bullying, aggression, or manipulation. People with poor self-esteem may be more inclined to employ aggressive strategies to gain attention or social authority, according to the review authors, who underline the need for additional research.

How to Develop Self-esteem

Your childhood experiences, such as love and nurture, rules and expectations, rewards and praise, influence your adult self-esteem. Lower self-esteem may increase your chances of:

- *Experience self-doubt.*
- *Use negative self-talk.*

- *Compare yourself to others and discover that you fall short.*
- *Possess people-pleasing and approval-seeking traits.*
- *Having difficulty setting limits with others.*
- *Encounter challenges in your interpersonal relationships.*

However, you can take action to recover and boost your self-esteem. These suggestions can help:

Pay attention to how you see yourself
Self-esteem is related to your impression of who you are, so think about how you see yourself. A more in-depth examination of your self-perception will help you begin to build your self-esteem.

To begin, you might spend some quiet time in deep thinking or journaling to unpack this question. Examining your self-beliefs can reveal more about your identity and areas where you might need to build your self-esteem.

Perhaps you feel incredibly happy when you achieve at work and extremely unhappy when you don't. You may then wonder why your self-esteem is affected by your job performance. What work-related beliefs have you adopted over time? Is there any evidence that supports them?

Create healthy relationships
Relationships, particularly familial ones, have an important role in the formation of self-esteem. As an adult, the people around you can either reaffirm or raise your self-esteem.

Making meaningful connections, whether with new or old friends, can assist in boosting your self-esteem. Higher self-esteem can help you sustain those relationships.

Wondering what makes a relationship healthy? Generally speaking, you will:

- *Feel safe discussing your views and feelings.*
- *Offer each other mutual emotional support.*
- *Manage disputes with love and respect.*

Practice positive self-talk
Paying attention to how you communicate with yourself might also have an impact. To assess your self-talk, consider whether you employ terms that encourage or discourage you. Would you be comfortable if someone spoke to your best friend in the same manner you spoke to yourself?

Negative self-talk can alter your perception of oneself, affecting both your mental health and your relationships with others. To reduce negative self-talk, you can:

Notice when it occurs and identify the thought
For example, "I'm useless since I botched up my presentation at work" or "This supper is a total disaster. Why did I bother? I can't perform anything correctly.

Challenge the thought with logic
For example, "Everyone makes mistakes; this does not make me a bad worker. Presenting may not be my strong suit, but I have a lot of other skills. Or, "So my culinary plans were a little grandiose, but I think I can salvage this. And if not, we can always joke about it and eat some pizza.

Repeat
When the concept arises again, answer using the same rationale.

The significance of treating yourself with compassion, which may include acknowledging and documenting your talents and accomplishments. This does not entail gushing and phony enthusiasm for yourself, but rather recognizing, in a journal or freewriting exercise, what you are actually good at.

Cultivate a growth attitude
If you have a fixed mindset, you may be hesitant to attempt new things. You may want to play it safe by sticking to what you know you are capable of, believing that attempting and failing would imply that you are a failure in your own right.

However, having a growth mindset allows you to recognize your ability to grow and learn, and you may feel more prepared to take on new tasks. When you focus on growth, you want to learn and perform your best.

This approach can also help you learn not to internalize your mistakes or use them to justify bad self-perceptions. Rather, you will most likely develop resilience and become more comfortable with new experiences.

Therapy
Connecting with a mental health expert can provide numerous benefits for developing self-esteem. A therapist can provide additional support with:

- *Identifying particular ideas causing poor self-esteem*
- *Recognize and break negative self-talk tendencies.*
- *Examining childhood situations that influenced your self-esteem*
- *Recognizing indications of healthy relationships*

According to 2018 research, cognitive behavioral therapy (CBT) may be especially effective for increasing self-esteem. Other options to examine are dialectical behavioral therapy (DBT) and psychodynamic therapy.

When to reach out
While a therapist may provide sympathetic counsel and support at any time, it's especially vital to get help if low self-esteem is affecting your life in more than one way. For example, if your self-esteem affects both your work performance and your social interactions, it may be time to seek professional help.

The bottom line
Everyone questions their confidence and ability from time to time, but if you generally feel good about yourself and your abilities, you undoubtedly have a high level of self-esteem.

If you regularly doubt yourself or struggle to identify any of your abilities or positive characteristics, you may have low self-esteem.

There is a lot you can do to change these perceptions and create a greater regard for yourself, which will improve your overall well-being as well as your relationships with others and yourself.

Chapter 6

Fostering Healthy Relationships

There is no relationship that is always healthy. A partnership is constantly a work in progress, which is where much of the beauty rests. However, there is a significant difference between flawed connections, which are normal, and those that are potentially abusive and could harm your life.

To identify the distinctions, consider other people's actions in relationships as green, red, or yellow flags. These adhere to the National Domestic Violence Hotline's definition of healthy, unhealthy, and abusive relationships.

Green Flags
These are positive practices that demonstrate respect and trust. People with several green flags should make you feel supported and cared for. These include open communication, emotional security, and mutual respect.

Red Flags
Red flags are warning signals that someone is manipulating or abusive, such as rude or threatening conversation, aggressive behavior, and attempts to control you. If these habits begin to emerge, consider ending the relationship or seeking professional treatment to address them.

Yellow Flags
These aren't definitely poisonous behavior patterns, but they are potentially harmful and should be monitored closely. Failure to communicate and unequal contributions to the relationship are examples of yellow flags.

If the person does not actively work on their yellow flags, they may develop into red flags, which is why it is critical to detect and communicate about them early on.

Pay attention to your relationships. How many green flags do you see? What about red? If you notice that the bad features are beginning to tilt the scale, take another look at the scenario. Talk to a good friend about whether the individual has a positive impact on your life or is holding you back.

Navigate Social Situations With Confidence

Personalized coaching can help you improve your social skills, boost your confidence, and form meaningful relationships.

You do not behave consistently in all of your relationships. Your parents and greatest friends get different forms of attention from you. Healthy relationships, however, follow a fairly constant set of basic rules, whether with your child or a close coworker. Here's what you should look for:

Earned Trust
You should be able to trust each other in a good relationship because you know you can rely on the other person for honesty and support. But no healthy relationship starts with perfect trust; you must prove and earn it. Building mutual trust is a long-term endeavor that demands commitment and perseverance.

Mutual Support
You and your significant other should support each other through difficult times, celebrate successes, and encourage each other to grow. You can put your own needs aside while they are struggling, and vice versa. This is also about communicating what support means to you.

Mature and healthy communication
Poor communication may be extremely damaging to relationships. One study discovered that married couples with higher amounts of negative communication were more likely to divorce within the first five years. Healthy relationships require a wide range of

communication skills, such as expressing gratitude, resolving conflict, and listening.

Respect
Respect in a relationship entails taking the time to understand the other person's boundaries and recognizing their talents and achievements.

Contempt is the reverse of respect
A perception that the other person is less valued, important, or intelligent than you. According to relationship researchers, disdain is the single most damaging conduct in a partnership.

Balance
In a balanced relationship, both partners make an effort, which varies depending on the situation. In a romantic partnership, balance usually refers to basic equality in terms of how much time and emotional labor each partner contributes.

In a hierarchical workplace relationship, there may not be equality, but there is reciprocity and recognition.

Honesty & Authenticity
Honesty entails expressing feelings in a straightforward, sympathetic manner without distorting or violating the truth. Similarly, authenticity means being honest about who you are. In a strong relationship, both partners have the freedom to exhibit their true personalities.

Affection and pleasant emotion
Being near another person should elevate your spirits and make you feel good, and affection demonstrates to them that you feel this way. And this communication does not have to be tangible. In the workplace, it could imply a friendly email welcome or a grin.

Tips For Developing Healthy Partnerships

A partnership is a mirror in which you may see yourself, not as you wish to be, but as you actually are. Relationships can bring out abilities you didn't know you had, but they can also reveal hidden faults and defects. That is why developing healthy relationships begins with reflection and self-awareness. Here's what you can do to cultivate good relationships and help those in your life:

Discover your core convictions
If you don't trust someone, it's possible that they've betrayed your confidence before or demonstrated a pattern of questionable conduct. Still, it can be an issue on your end. Your underlying beliefs and previous experiences may cause you to perceive betrayal even when none exists. Exploring these underlying beliefs and developing self-awareness prepares you to approach relationships in an informed and wise manner.

Cherish each other's vulnerabilities
In the early stages of a relationship, you may wish to project your best self while concealing your fears. But after a while, you begin to open up and reveal who you truly are. When someone is vulnerable with you, show them they can trust you by avoiding jokes and unpleasant comments. Show your support and concern.

Ask for aid when you need it
Asking for assistance is difficult. However, healthy partnerships include both giving and receiving. When you seek help from someone, whether emotional or otherwise, you are giving them the option to support you, and chances are they will gladly accept it. This also demonstrates to the other individual that they should feel safe doing the same when the necessity arises.

Protect your relationship from stress
Stressed-out individuals have little energy left over for their relationships, so continual stress can wear out your ties over time, whether through internal conflict or external suffering. One way to avoid this is to discuss previous struggles as battles that you

overcame together. This approach is known by researchers as "glorifying the struggle."

Show appreciation
Expressing thankfulness is a simple method to increase relationship pleasure. In fact, it may even set off a virtuous cycle in which receiving praise makes you more likely to appreciate your mate. Find and take advantage of opportunities to express gratitude, whether through nice words or a gesture of thanks.

Set aside time to discuss your hopes and anxieties
The infatuation during the start of a love relationship is high in happy hormones. However, such intensity can wear off with time. Make an effort to keep learning about each other and instilling feelings of newness and excitement. Hopes, anxieties, and plans evolve throughout time, so have regular conversations to keep on track and find new things you enjoy.

Fight with intention
Conflict is quite powerful. It can either break or strengthen relationships. However, resolving disputes maturely can be exceedingly challenging, particularly if you are defensive. Show that you care by acknowledging the other person's need, even if you disagree with it, and focusing on constructive solutions.

Listen actively and attempt to perceive the conflict not as you versus the other person, but as you and the other person versus the problem. If one of you feels overwhelmed by emotion, pause and take a break. Allowing oneself time for emotional control can provide the insight you need to handle the problem constructively.

Embrace your differences
Everyone's personality is distinct and evolves with time, so you and others around you will always have differences. Acknowledge your weaknesses and areas of skill complementation on a regular basis, and respect each other's contributions to the partnership.

Communicate and keep healthy boundaries
Try to communicate your limits proactively, whether they are about how much time you can spend with someone or your level of emotional intimacy. However, sometimes you only become aware of a boundary after someone crosses it, so if they do anything you are uncomfortable with, explain it plainly.

In the same spirit, pay attention to any signs that the other person is establishing limits, no matter how subtle they are. Don't be hesitant to clarify verbally and ask what they expect from you. Healthy partnerships, friendships, and familial interactions provide opportunities to discuss limits.

Check in regularly
Even in healthy relationships, you will occasionally fail to communicate. If you are ill or have a busy schedule, you may not pay attention or realize you are neglecting someone. Check in with the other person on a frequent basis to see how they're doing, what they're working on, and if there's anything you can do to help.

Be a good listener
Listening fosters a sense of community and encourages creative thinking. If you can listen actively and without judgment, you will be able to develop your relationships and handle difficulties more effectively.

When it comes to disputes, listening to the other person does not need you to change your mind or even agree. But it will help you understand and connect with them, allowing you to establish common ground.

Learn how you prefer to offer and receive affection
People enjoy receiving affection in five ways: acts of service, gifts, quality time, words of affirmation, and physical touch. You may feel good when your friend verbally compliments you, whereas your friend may feel good when you engage in an activity together, such as going for a stroll. That suggests your love language is words of affirmation, whereas your friend's is quality time.

If you don't know how you prefer to receive affection or how to express your sentiments, take a love language quiz. Then you can give individuals the attention and effort they deserve, in the way they want it.

Have fun together
Strong relationships need effort, but they should not feel like labor all the time. Schedule time to explore, try new things and engage in activities that both you and the person you care about enjoy. Spending your leisure time working on your relationship demonstrates that you are both enthusiastic and willing to put forth the effort.

Improving a relationship and figuring out what works for both of you is a wonderful thing. However, in certain situations, being patient and waiting for change might backfire. Accepting someone for who they are sometimes involves acknowledging that they will never meet your demands, which may result in the end of the relationship.

Whether you're no longer friends with a coworker or are splitting up with a long-term partner, the process of terminating a relationship can be challenging and heartbreaking. The people in your life will always be in flux, no matter what stage of life you're in, but it doesn't make time away from them any easier.

Be honest, communicate, and take care of yourself. Also, don't forget about the folks you already have. They contribute more to your overall well-being than you realize.

In relational health, as in physical health, avoiding disaster is considerably more valuable than treating it. Be proactive, and don't wait for a problem to arise before putting in the work. In healthy relationships, there is always more to learn and grow, and actively working on your connections will benefit both you and others you care about.

Conclusion

Navigating the realm of manipulation might feel like attempting to navigate your way through a maze while blindfolded. Manipulators have a way of manipulating situations and words to their advantage, leaving you bewildered and disoriented.

What if you were able to defeat them in their own match? What if you had a toolkit full of tactics for not only avoiding manipulation but also for encouraging healthier and more real interactions?

These are not about descending to the level of manipulators, but about elevating the debate to one of authenticity and respect. Let's go into this empowering trip.

Developing self-awareness
Self-awareness is the ability to identify one's own emotions, reactions, and behaviors. It's important to understand what triggers you and how you respond to those stimuli. It's about being able to step back, watch the event objectively, and recognize your role in it.

When you're self-aware, you'll see trends. For example, does the manipulator constantly flatter you when they need something? Or perhaps they use guilt-tripping when they feel threatened?

Recognizing these patterns allows you to predict the manipulator's tactics and avoid being affected by them. You may make judgments based on your values and priorities rather than becoming entangled in their web.

Accepting the power of assertiveness
Assertiveness is an effective skill for dealing with manipulation. It is not about being aggressive or belligerent, but about asserting your rights and communicating your views, feelings, and demands in a straightforward, honest, and acceptable manner.

For most of my life, I struggled with assertiveness. I was frightened of provoking confrontation, upsetting others, and not being loved.

But, over time, I recognized that by avoiding these uncomfortable situations, I was actually promoting manipulative practices. Assertiveness starts with straightforward communication. It demands you to define your boundaries and stick to them even when they are challenged. It also entails understanding and respecting other people's rights, as well as striking a balance between giving and receiving.

Mastering assertiveness entails remaining cool in the face of adversity and standing firm with grace rather than grit. You owe no apologies for your limits, no guilt for your 'no's, and no concessions for your wishes and requirements.

Building resilience in the face of setbacks
Navigating life's challenges can sometimes feel like an uphill battle, especially when dealing with deceitful people. However, resilience is more than just weathering the storm; it is about learning and evolving from these challenges.

Being resilient necessitates an attitude adjustment. Instead of perceiving setbacks as indicators of failure, consider their chances for growth and learning. This reframe can enable us to recover from difficult experiences with greater strength and insight.

One important feature of resilience is adaptability. When you can adjust to shifting conditions, you are less likely to be caught off guard by the manipulator's tactics. You can keep your cool and make judgments based on your values rather than being swept up in the frenzy.

Aligning actions and core principles
In a society full of manipulation and dishonesty, it's easy to lose sight of who we are and what we believe in. This is why, when dealing with manipulators, we must connect our behaviors with our underlying principles.

Values serve as a compass in our lives, directing our decisions and behaviors. When we realize what is most important to us, it is simpler to stay firm against manipulation. It's easier to say "no" when something doesn't line with our beliefs, and "yes" when they do.

However, it is easier said than done. Living our ideals demands courage and integrity. It entails deciding to do what is right, even if it is difficult or inconvenient. It entails sticking up for ourselves and our beliefs, especially when we face adversity.

This strategy is not about winning or losing to the manipulator. It's about remaining loyal to ourselves while maintaining our dignity and self-worth.

Fostering genuine partnerships
In a society full of manipulation, it's tempting to become cynical and isolate ourselves. However, this method frequently leaves us feeling isolated and detached. Instead, I believe that cultivating honest relationships is extremely important.

Authentic relationships are built on mutual respect, empathy, and collaboration. They are connections in which we may express ourselves freely, without fear of being judged or rejected. They are partnerships that enhance our lives, push us to grow, and offer us encouragement and company.

However, developing honest relationships is not always simple. Setting limits calls for vulnerability, honesty, and courage. It requires us to remove our masks and expose our actual selves, even if it is uncomfortable or dangerous.

Let this serve as a continual reminder: the quality of our relationships frequently dictates the quality of our lives. The more genuine our interactions are, the more fulfilled and content we tend to be.

Releasing the demand for control
When dealing with manipulators, we typically have a strong desire to regain control. It seems logical, doesn't it? After all, the manipulator is attempting to dominate us, so it seems only reasonable that we fight back and attempt to regain control.

However, this can become a trap. The more we try to gain control, the more enmeshed we become in the manipulator's web. Similar to quicksand, the more we try, the more we sink.

Rather, I suggest a different strategy: letting go of the need for control. This does not mean becoming passive or submissive. It does not imply that we should let the manipulator get away with everything. Rather, it is about knowing what we can and cannot control.

We have no influence over the manipulator's behavior or attitudes. We can't make them change or treat us differently. Our responses, however, are under our control.

Practicing empathy without getting involved
Empathy is frequently interpreted as a vulnerability in the face of manipulation. After all, manipulators are known to prey on empathic people, taking advantage of their sympathy and empathy.

Empathy, on the other hand, does not necessarily imply weakness. When used correctly, it can be an effective tool for navigational manipulation. Empathy permits us to comprehend the manipulator's viewpoint, goals, and strategies. This understanding can provide us with significant insights into how to interact with them effectively while avoiding becoming entangled in their web.

However, empathy does not imply approving or endorsing the manipulator's behavior. It does not imply allowing oneself to be used or abused. Rather, it is about preserving emotional equilibrium and responding to manipulation in a conscious and educated manner.

Investing in personal growth and awareness
The third method for fighting manipulators at their own game is possibly the most important: invest in personal growth and self-awareness.

Personal development entails facing our anxieties, changing our limiting beliefs, and developing self-compassion. It is about becoming more self-aware and conscious of our thoughts, feelings, and behaviors.

Individuals become more resistant to manipulation as they grow and evolve. We gain a higher sense of self-worth and confidence. We learn how to set limits and stand up for ourselves. We improve our ability to recognize and respond effectively to manipulation.

Investing in personal development entails broadening our knowledge and awareness of manipulative techniques. This provides us with the tools we need to detect and successfully counter manipulation when it occurs.

As we investigate the complex dynamics of human interactions and behavior, it's fascinating to study the role of conscious choices in shaping our experiences.

Every time we encounter a manipulator, we are presented with a decision. We can let them control our reactions and emotions, or we can respond consciously, guided by our principles and self-awareness.

This is more than just a psychological phenomenon; it's a tremendous demonstration of our ability to control our own lives. It is about acknowledging our own agency and using it to overcome difficult situations with perseverance and dignity.

How would our interactions alter if we saw each contact with a manipulator as a chance for growth and learning? How would it feel to know that whatever techniques they use, we have the tools and power to respond intelligently and effectively?

Made in United States
North Haven, CT
27 October 2025